Slavery in
the United States

BY
CINDY BARDEN

COPYRIGHT © 2002 Mark Twain Media, Inc.

ISBN 1-58037-185-X

Printing No. CD-1531

Mark Twain Media, Inc., Publishers
Distributed by Carson-Dellosa Publishing Company, Inc.

Table of Contents

About the American History Series

Welcome to *Slavery in the United States,* one of 12 books in the Mark Twain Media, Inc., American History series for students in grades four to seven.

The activity books in this series are designed as stand-alone material for classrooms and home-schoolers or as supplemental material to enhance your history curriculum. Students can be encouraged to use the books as independent study units to improve their understanding of historical events and people.

Each book provides challenging activities that enable students to explore history, geography, and social studies topics. The activities provide research opportunities and promote critical reading, thinking, and writing skills. As students follow the crusade to abolish slavery and learn about the people who influenced this turbulent period in history, they will draw conclusions; write opinions; compare and contrast historical events, people, and places; analyze cause and effect; and improve mapping skills. Students will also have the opportunity to apply what they learn to their own lives through reflection and creative writing.

Students can further increase their knowledge and understanding of historical events by using reference sources at the library and on the Internet. Students may need assistance to learn how to use search engines and discover appropriate websites.

Titles of books for additional reading appropriate to the subject matter at this grade level are included in each book.

Although many of the questions are open-ended, answer keys are included at the back of the book for questions with specific answers.

Share a journey through history with your students as you explore the books in the Mark Twain Media, Inc., American History series:

Discovering and Exploring the Americas
Life in the Colonies
The American Revolution
The Lewis and Clark Expedition
The Westward Movement
The California Gold Rush
The Oregon and Santa Fe Trails
Slavery in the United States
The American Civil War
Abraham Lincoln and His Times
The Reconstruction Era
Industrialization in America

Time Line of *Slavery in the United States*

1619	The first slaves were brought to Jamestown colony by a Dutch trader.
1634	The first African slaves were imported to Maryland and Massachusetts.
1638	The first American slave auction was held in Jamestown.
1641	The Massachusetts colony legalized slavery.
1642	Virginia law: Anyone who assisted a runaway slave would be fined.
1650	The Connecticut colony legalized slavery.
1661	Virginia legalized slavery.
1662	Virginia law: Any child born of a slave mother would also be a slave.
1663	Maryland law: If a free White woman married a slave, she and their children would be slaves for life.
1681	Maryland law: Children born to free White women and male slaves would be free.
1688	The first formal protest of slavery in the Americas was signed by Pennsylvania Quakers.
1691	Virginia law: Interracial marriage was prohibited.
1776	The Declaration of Independence was signed.
1777	Vermont abolished slavery.
1780	Pennsylvania abolished slavery.
1781	Black soldiers participated in the defeat of Cornwallis at Yorktown.
	The Massachusetts court awarded freedom to Elizabeth Freeman.
1783	Slavery was abolished in Massachusetts and New Hampshire.
1784	Slavery was abolished in Connecticut and Rhode Island.
1785	New York passed a law against selling any new slaves in the state or selling any New York slave out of state.
1786	The importation of new slaves ended in all states except Georgia and South Carolina.
1787	Slavery was prohibited in the Northwest Territory.
	The U.S. Constitution was written.
1788	British law restricted the number of slaves carried by a ship, based on the ship's tonnage.
	French abolitionists founded the Society of the Friends of Blacks.
1789	The Maryland Abolitionist Society was founded.

Time Line of *Slavery in the United States*

1791	The Imperial Act outlawed the importation of slaves into Upper Canada.
	Slaves revolted in Haiti.
1793	The first federal Fugitive Slave Act made it illegal to assist runaway slaves.
1794	France freed all slaves in the French colonies.
1803	Denmark banned slave trading.
1804	New Jersey abolished slavery.
1807	The British Parliament prohibited British subjects from engaging in the slave trade after March 1, 1808.
1808	The importation of slaves into the United States became illegal.
1811	Slave trading became a felony punishable by exile to a penal colony for anyone trading in British territory.
1812	Louisiana became a state.
1816	Indiana became a state.
1817	New York abolished slavery.
	Mississippi became a state.
1818	Slave trading became illegal in Holland and France.
	Illinois became a state.
1820	The Missouri Compromise was passed to maintain the balance of free and slave states.
	Maine became a state.
1821	Missouri became a state.
1828	Andrew Jackson was elected president.
1831	A major slave revolt occurred in Jamaica.
	William Lloyd Garrison founded the antislavery newspaper, *The Liberator*.
1834	The Abolition Act freed slaves in the British West Indies.
1836	Portugal banned slave trade.
	Arkansas became a state.
1837	Michigan became a state.
1840	William Henry Harrison was elected president.
1841	William Henry Harrison died; John Tyler became president.
1844	James K. Polk was elected president.
1845	Florida and Texas became states.

Time Line of *Slavery in the United States*

1846   Iowa became a state.

1848   The United States gained Arizona, California, Nevada, New Mexico, Utah, and western Colorado from Mexico after the Mexican War in exchange for $15 million.

Zachary Taylor was elected president.

Wisconsin became a state.

1850   President Zachary Taylor died; Millard Fillmore became president.

California became a state.

1852   Franklin Pierce was elected president.

1853   The Gadsden Purchase was acquired from Mexico for $10 million.

1856   James Buchanan was elected president.

1857   Supreme Court rules in the Dred Scott case.

1858   Minnesota became a state.

1859   Oregon became a state.

1860   Abraham Lincoln was elected president.

1861   The Civil War began.

Kansas became a state.

1863   Lincoln issued the Emancipation Proclamation.

West Virginia became a state.

1864   President Lincoln was reelected.

Nevada became a state.

1865   President Lincoln was assassinated; Andrew Johnson became president.

1867   Alaska was purchased from Russia for $7.2 million in gold.

Nebraska became a state.

1868   Ulysses S. Grant was elected president.

1869   The Transcontinental Railroad was completed.

1872   President Grant was reelected.

1888   Slavery was abolished in Brazil.

Name:_____ Date: _____

A Historical View of Slavery

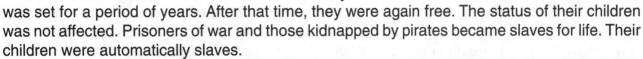

Slavery did not begin when the first Dutch ship exchanged a cargo of African slaves for food at the Jamestown colony in 1619, nor did it end when slavery was finally abolished in the United States 246 years later.

Slavery has been part of human history since the earliest times. People in ancient China, India, Mesopotamia, Egypt, Greece, and Rome owned slaves. In South America, the Aztecs, Incas, and Mayas practiced slavery. People in other parts of the world also owned slaves and forced them to work without any pay or benefits.

Some people were forced into slavery as a form of punishment because they committed crimes or fell into debt. In these cases, the term of slavery was set for a period of years. After that time, they were again free. The status of their children was not affected. Prisoners of war and those kidnapped by pirates became slaves for life. Their children were automatically slaves.

The first known incident of slavery of Africans by Europeans occurred when ten African slaves were kidnapped by a Portuguese trader in 1441 and taken back to Portugal. Kidnapping as a way of obtaining slaves continued for a time, but this soon led to retribution by African leaders.

Portuguese traders found they could trade horses, silks, and silver for slaves. Since slavery was common in Africa, leaders saw no reason not to trade slaves for goods with the Europeans. Spain, Portugal, the Netherlands, and other European countries began trading with the people of several great empires (Mali, Benin, Dahomey, and Kongo) along the coast of Africa.

By 1448, there were about a thousand slaves in Portugal, mainly used for agricultural work. The Spanish quickly followed the example of the Portuguese, importing slaves to work in their colonies in the New World.

1. If slavery is legal, do you think that makes it right? Why or why not?

    _____

    _____

    _____

2. What do you think of slavery as a form of punishment for crimes?

    _____

    _____

    _____

3. Use a dictionary. Define *retribution*. _____

    _____

5

Name:_____ Date: _____

Europe and Slavery

Spain and Portugal were the first European nations to engage in the African slave trade. France, Holland, and Denmark also actively bought and sold African slaves. Slaves were taken from Africa to Europe where they were either sold or shipped to the New World for sale.

When Europeans began developing the resources of the Americas, they needed huge amounts of cheap labor. The Spanish and Portuguese forced large numbers of African slaves to work the gold and silver mines and the large sugarcane plantations in Mexico, Central and South America, and the Caribbean Islands.

Not all slaves in the American colonies were Africans. Early in the 1700s, about 25 percent of slaves in colonies such as the Carolinas were Native Americans. From the 1500s through the early 1700s, a small number of White people were also enslaved.

The first African slaves in America were taken to the English colony of Jamestown in 1619. British colonists in both the North and the South owned slaves, but England did not take an active part in procuring slaves until after 1650. Eventually the British dominated the slave trade.

An Englishman, Sir John Hawkins, came up with the most efficient way of trading African slaves for profit. From England, his ships sailed to the west coast of Africa where they traded goods for slaves. Then they sailed directly to North America where the slaves were sold or exchanged for goods made in the New World. Those goods were taken back to England and sold for a profit.

Soon other European nations followed this profitable **triangular trade route**. The second part of the voyage, from Africa to the Americas, came to be called the **Middle Passage**.

At least 10 million Africans were forced into slavery between the fifteenth and nineteenth centuries. Some scholars estimate even higher numbers.

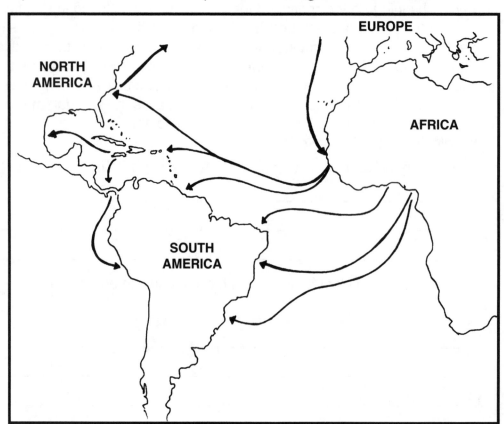

Name:_____ Date:_____

Life Aboard a Slave Ship

Groups of slaves captured in the interior of Africa were forced to march hundreds of miles to the coast. To prevent escape, chains were passed through loops in iron or wooden collars around their necks and through iron cuffs around their wrists and ankles to keep slaves chained together. Often they were forced to carry heavy burdens as they traveled. Any slave attempting to escape would be severely beaten or killed.

When they reached the coast, the slaves were imprisoned until they were sold. The most desirable slaves were males between the ages of 15 and 25. At Fort Elmina in Ghana, up to a thousand slaves could be held in stone dungeons. In Angola, captives were penned in open stockades.

After examining the slaves and agreeing on a purchase price, slave traders usually branded the slaves with a hot iron to show ownership and returned them to the pens until they had purchased enough slaves to fill their ships.

When they were ready to sail, slave traders herded the captives onto their ships for the five-week journey across the Atlantic. The slaves were crowded into small spaces below deck and forced to remain during most of the journey, often chained to each other or to wooden beams.

Water was seldom available for washing. Ventilation was poor. Wooden buckets were used as toilets. It was claimed that the odor of a slave ship could be smelled five miles away. Conditions on ships were so dirty, many captives died of diseases. Because of the crowded conditions, diseases often spread quickly.

Slaves were usually brought up on deck and fed twice a day. Meals consisted of porridge or beans and water. When the weather was good, slaves might be taken on deck to exercise. This was done to keep the slaves as healthy as possible, because healthy slaves were worth more when sold.

Circle the words that best describe the conditions on a slave ship. Use a dictionary if you are unsure of the meaning of a word.

inhumane	sanitary
adventurous	filthy
gentle	cruel
benevolent	wonderful
terrifying	humane
atrocious	dreadful

Name:_____ Date: _____

The Legal Status of Slaves

Although each colony enacted its own laws regarding slavery, by the 1680s, the laws in most colonies were quite similar. Slaves were not recognized as persons by law; therefore, they had no legal rights.

Slavery was a permanent condition inherited through the mother. Slaves were considered property. They could be bought, sold, punished, or loaned to someone else in the same way a person might loan a neighbor a shovel or a mule.

Like other forms of property, slaves could be passed on to others in a will or given away.

Slaves could not own any property, serve as witnesses in a court, serve on juries, or make contracts. Since marriage is a contract, no slave marriage was considered legal.

Even freed slaves were restricted by laws that controlled their travel, employment, and legal status. In many states, a freed slave was required to leave the state.

Slaves charged with crimes in Virginia were tried in a special court. They had no rights to trial by jury. The purpose of the trial was not to seek justice, but to set an example for other slaves by imposing terrible punishments that could include whipping, branding, hanging, and being burnt at a stake.

1. What rights do you think your bike or VCR have? _____

2. What rights do you think your pets or other animals have? _____

   _____

3. How do you think the fact that slaves were treated like property made slaves feel about themselves?

   _____

   _____

4. Do you think slaves were treated more like objects or animals? Explain your answer.

   _____

   _____

   _____

5. Why do you think a freed slave would be required to leave the state? _____

   _____

   _____

6. Which right that you have do you think is the most important? Why?

   _____

   _____

   _____

Name:_____ Date:_____

Slavery in the South

Although most people think of White Southerners in the 1700s and 1800s as slave owners, only one in four Southern families actually owned slaves. Three-quarters of Southern families did not own slaves.

Not all Blacks in the South were slaves, either. By the time the Civil War began in 1861, about 25 percent of the Blacks in the South were free. Most free Blacks in the South weren't much better off than slaves, but in some areas they were allowed to marry, own property, attend schools, and even own slaves.

Most movies and books show hundreds of slaves working on huge plantations, but that isn't a complete picture. Only about 30,000 Southerners owned 50 or more slaves. Most Southerners who owned slaves lived and worked on smaller farms and in cities. Slaves not only worked in agriculture, but they also worked in shipyards, businesses, and as house slaves.

Slavery was an economic institution in the South. Cheap labor was needed to work the fields of cotton and tobacco. With the invention of the cotton gin in 1793, the cost of producing cotton was cut, and the demand for cotton cloth increased. Growing more cotton meant the need for even more workers.

Those who owned large plantations and many slaves were from the wealthiest families. They sought to maintain their wealth by controlling the source of their wealth—cotton, slaves, and all laws regarding slavery.

Unlike other societies, slavery in the South was not based on forcing prisoners of war to be slaves. Slavery was based on race. Europeans believed that Africans were inferior, suited by their character and circumstances to be slaves forever. This attitude remained most strongly in the South, long after Europe abolished slavery and the slave trade.

Use reference sources or the Internet to answer the following questions.

1. Who invented the cotton gin? _____

2. What did the cotton gin do? _____

   _____

   _____

3. What is racism? _____

   _____

4. On your own paper, answer the following question: Do you think racism still exists in the United States today? Give an example to support your answer.

Name:_____ Date:_____

Slavery in the North

Slavery was not unique to the Southern colonies. The Dutch imported slaves to New Amsterdam to work on farms in the Hudson Valley. According to Dutch law, children of freed slaves were still legally slaves.

Other Europeans who settled in the Northern colonies of the New World kept slaves to work in their homes, on farms, and in businesses. Most shipowners and sea captains involved in the slave trade were Northerners. Several Northern coastal cities became centers for slave traffic.

Although never very widespread north of Delaware, slavery did exist in every American colony until the Revolutionary War. Slavery ended in Vermont in 1777. New York was the last Northern state to abolish slavery in 1817.

Even after slavery became illegal in the North, the lives of free Blacks were very difficult. Whites, especially recent immigrants, feared Blacks would take over jobs, leaving them unemployed. Mobs rampaged through areas where Blacks lived and worked in Ohio and New York. Many Blacks fled to Canada.

White rioters in Philadelphia in 1834 and 1842 destroyed Black churches, attacked Black men and women on the streets, and burned their homes. In some states, federal troops were needed to stop the violence.

Schools that allowed Black students to attend were destroyed in several Northern states. In Canterbury, Connecticut, a woman who ran a private school admitted Black girls. Shop owners refused to sell her supplies, and neighbors tried to poison her well. When she persisted, she was ordered to close the school and was arrested. The school building was destroyed.

The attitude towards slavery in the North was very mixed. Not every Northerner believed slaves should be free or that Blacks deserved equal rights.

1. Imagine being the mayor of a large Northern city. Mobs of White people are rampaging through your city, attacking Blacks, and destroying their homes. What would you do?

   _____

   _____

   _____

   _____

2. If you had run a private school in the North in the early 1800s, would you have allowed Black students to attend? Why or why not?

   _____

   _____

   _____

   _____

Name:_____ Date:_____

The Declaration of Independence

When representatives of the American colonies met to form a new nation and declare their freedom from Great Britain, they considered many issues, including slavery.

Thomas Jefferson (a slave owner from Virginia) included ideas from members of the Continental Congress as well as his own ideas about freedom to write the Declaration of Independence. In the first draft, he included a provision that abolished slavery. That section was deleted by the Continental Congress before it was signed in 1776.

The first section of the Declaration of Independence includes these words:

JULY 4, 1776

> "We hold these truths to be self-evident, that all men are created equal, that they are endowed by their Creator with certain unalienable Rights, that among these are Life, Liberty, and the pursuit of Happiness …"

The phrase "all men" did not include African-Americans or Native American men. The Declaration of Independence also excluded all women of every race and nationality.

The men who wrote the Declaration of Independence believed that men had the right to own property. Since slaves were considered property, and property had no rights, there was no reason to include any rights for slaves.

Another section at the beginning of this famous document states that if any form of government does not grant life, liberty, and the pursuit of happiness to the people, they have the right to change or abolish the government and to form a new one that provides for their safety and happiness.

1. Use a dictionary. Define *unalienable* (now *inalienable*). _____

   _____

2. Use a dictionary. Define *endowed*. _____

   _____

3. If you had been a Black slave at that time, how would you have felt about the Declaration of Independence? Be specific.

   _____

   _____

   _____

   _____

Name:_____ Date:_____

The Constitution of the United States

After the Revolutionary War, the leaders of the new nation met again to write a Constitution in 1787. They did not seriously consider abolishing slavery in the Constitution. If they had, most of the delegates from the Southern states would have refused to sign, and the Southern states would have refused to ratify it.

The delegates felt it was more important to put together a strong new nation than to deal with the difficult and controversial issue of slavery. There were also many other issues besides slavery that needed to be resolved. Many compromises were made before the final draft of the Constitution was approved. Those dealing with slavery were known as the Great Compromise.

Even though the words *slave* and *slavery* do not appear in the Constitution, that document included ten provisions dealing with the issue. In the final version, the United States government could not abolish the importation of new slaves for 20 years, and slave owners had the right to capture runaway slaves, even in Northern states.

Another important issue regarded representation of the states in Congress. Large states wanted more power, based on population. Small states wanted equal representation. In the Constitution, all states received equal representation in the Senate, and the number of members of the House of Representatives was based on population.

This made it necessary for another compromise. Although the Southern states refused to consider Blacks as people, they wanted them included in the total population. In the end, it was agreed that for representation in Congress, each slave would be counted as $\frac{3}{5}$ of a person.

1. Use a dictionary. Define *controversial.* _____

    _____

2. Use a dictionary. Define *compromise.* _____

    _____

3. Write your opinion of the compromises made in the Constitution. _____

    _____

    _____

    _____

    _____

    _____

    _____

Name:_____ Date:_____

Meet Phillis Wheatley

Phillis Wheatley was captured by slave traders when she was about seven or eight years old. She was taken from Africa in a slave ship in 1761 and sold at an auction. John and Susannah Wheatley of Boston purchased her.

After Phillis learned to speak English, the Wheatleys allowed their daughter Mary to teach her to read and write. They read the Bible and poetry together. Soon Phillis began writing her own poetry.

When Phillis was about 17, Mrs. Wheatley gathered some of her poetry for a book, which was published in England in 1773. The book was very popular, and she was invited to England. Phillis traveled there with the Wheatleys' son, John. In England, she was a popular guest in literary circles.

Phillis stayed in England until she received a letter from Mary Wheatley telling her that Mrs. Wheatley was very ill. Mary asked Phillis to return to Boston. After

Phillis Wheatley was the first Black woman in America to have her poetry published. She is remembered as "the mother of Black literature in America."

she returned from England, the Wheatleys set her free. Phillis continued to live with them until Mr. and Mrs. Wheatley died.

"I was treated by her more like her child than her servant," Phillis wrote to a friend after Mrs. Wheatley died.

When the Revolutionary War began, Phillis wrote a poem about George Washington and sent it to him with a letter. Although busy with the war, he invited her to visit him at his headquarters in Cambridge, Massachusetts.

Phillis married a free Black man, John Peters, but their life was difficult. Because of money problems, John was sent to jail. Phillis had three children, but they all died as babies.

Phillis herself died on December 5, 1784. Her best-known poems are "To the University of Cambridge in New England" and "To the King's Most Excellent Majesty."

Read a poem by Phillis Wheatley and rewrite one verse in your own words.

_____

_____

_____

_____

_____

_____

_____

Name:_____ Date:_____

The Fugitive Slave Laws

Ever since people were first forced into slavery, they sought ways to escape their bondage. In the United States, slaves from Southern states fled to Northern states or to Canada where slavery was illegal. Southerners objected when slaves escaped because they were losing "valuable property."

The federal Fugitive Slave Laws in the United States made it easier for slave owners to return runaways back to their homes, even if they were captured in a state where slavery was illegal. These laws reinforced the commitment of the federal government in the belief that slaves were property.

The Fugitive Slave Law of 1793 allowed slave owners or their agents to capture fugitives in any state or territory. "Slave-catchers," professional bounty hunters who hunted for, captured, and returned runaway slaves to their masters, were often hampered by Whites in Northern cities.

Northerners objected to this law, because they felt it violated civil liberties. As more Northern states abolished slavery, many believed that once a slave entered a free state, he or she should automatically be free. They also felt the law offered too little protection for freed slaves, who were often kidnapped and sold back into slavery.

Slave owners felt the law wasn't strong enough. There were no penalties for helping a slave escape or harboring a fugitive. They believed the federal law violated the rights of states to make their own laws regarding property.

The Fugitive Slave Law of 1850 made it mandatory for federal marshals to assist in recapturing runaways. It also penalized anyone helping a slave escape; penalties included fines and imprisonment for up to six months.

1. Use a dictionary. What does *fugitive* mean? _____

_____

2. If you knew you might be caught and sent to prison, would you have helped a slave escape? Why or why not?

_____

_____

_____

_____

_____

Name:_____ Date:_____

Meet Elizabeth Freeman

Elizabeth was born around 1742. When she was about six months old, Elizabeth and her sister Lizzie were purchased by Colonel John Ashley of Ashley Falls, Massachusetts. Elizabeth worked in his kitchen and gardens. She often heard her master and his guests talk about freedom and independence from England.

Her husband fought and died for freedom in the Revolutionary War. Elizabeth heard Colonel Ashley read the Declaration of Independence. However, she discovered that the words "... all men are created equal ..." did not include her or the other slaves.

In 1780 Elizabeth learned that the state constitution of Massachusetts declared that "All men are born free and equal." She felt that should apply to slaves also.

Although she and Colonel Ashley's other slaves were treated far better than slaves in many areas, Mrs. Ashley was stern and demanded that they work hard. She punished those who did not.

One day, Mrs. Ashley grabbed a hot shovel from the fireplace and was about to hit Lizzie with it when Elizabeth stepped in front of her sister to protect her. The shovel hit her instead. Angry, Elizabeth took her baby and left with another slave named Brom.

Elizabeth asked Theodore Sedgwick, a young lawyer, to take their case to court. She wanted her sister to join them, but Lizzie was too afraid to stand up for her rights and remained with the Ashleys.

1. Why do you think accepting a case like this might have caused Sedgwick trouble?

   _____

   _____

   _____

2. If you had been Theodore Sedgwick, would you have taken the case? Why or why not?

   _____

   _____

   _____

3. How was Elizabeth's life as a slave similar to Phillis Wheatley's?

   _____

   _____

   _____

Name:_____ Date:_____

The Case Goes to Court

Theodore Sedgwick agreed to represent Elizabeth and Brom in court. Although Mrs. Ashley apologized, and Mr. Ashley asked them to return, they refused. Brom went to work on a farm, and Elizabeth agreed to work for Mr. Sedgwick until the case could be heard in court.

When they went to court in August 1781, there were many arguments from both sides. Mr. Ashley claimed that Elizabeth and the other slaves were his legal servants for life.

The jury reached a different decision. Elizabeth and Brom became the first slaves freed under Massachusetts law. The court also ordered Colonel Ashley to pay them 30 shillings (for past wages) and court costs.

For the rest of her life Elizabeth worked for Theodore Sedgwick, taking care of his home and children. When she died, Theodore's youngest son, Charles, wrote the words engraved on her tombstone:

Elizabeth Freeman
known by the name of Mumbet
died December 28, 1829
Her supposed age was 85 Years.

"She was born a slave and remained a slave for nearly thirty years. She could neither read nor write yet in her own sphere she had no superior nor equal. She neither wasted time nor property. She never violated a trust nor failed to perform a duty. In every situation of domestic trial, she was the most efficient helper and the tenderest friend. Good mother farewell."

This case was one of the most important slave cases in Massachusetts in 1781 and ultimately led to the abolition of slavery in that state two years later.

1. After reading about the *Dred Scott* Decision on page 27, compare the two cases. How were they similar?

    _____

    _____

    _____

    _____

2. Why do you think the verdicts were so different?

    _____

    _____

    _____

    _____

Name:_____ Date:_____

The Beginning of the Abolitionist Movement

Abolitionists were people who wanted to end slavery. The Society of Friends (Quakers) of Pennsylvania were the earliest group in America to protest slavery. In 1688 they published an antislavery resolution.

Many abolitionists believed they could convince others of the evils of slavery by publishing newspapers, almanacs, and books. Abolitionist societies sponsored lectures and invited former slaves like Frederick Douglass and Sojourner Truth to speak at their meetings. They hoped that hearing about the horrors of slavery from people who had been slaves would convince the audience to take action.

In the 1840s, abolitionist societies used songs to stir up enthusiasm at their meetings. To make the songs easier to learn, new words were often set to familiar tunes.

At times, abolitionist speakers found audiences interested in hearing their message. Sometimes, however, the audience responded to those who spoke out against slavery by throwing rotten eggs or rocks. Elijah Lovejoy, the publisher of an abolitionist newspaper in Alton, Illinois, was killed by a proslavery mob.

Many abolitionists wanted to end slavery peacefully by legal means through religious and political pressure. They wanted to make people aware of the evils of slavery so that the laws permitting slavery would be repealed.

Even though they wanted to end slavery legally, many became conductors on the Underground Railroad, helping runaway slaves escape. Since any assistance of runaway slaves was illegal under the Fugitive Slave Laws, they were technically criminals.

1. Do you think music is a good way to get across a message? Why or why not?

   _____

   _____

   _____

2. Do you think the peaceful method would have worked to abolish slavery? Why or why not?

   _____

   _____

   _____

3. Do you think conductors on the Underground Railroad were criminals? Why or why not?

   _____

   _____

   _____

Name:_____ Date:_____

The Abolitionist Movement Grows

Although many people believed slavery was wrong, they did not believe Blacks should have equal rights. They wanted them to be free from slavery, but not to attend the same schools and churches or live in the same neighborhoods. Their solution was to free all slaves and return them to Africa.

William Lloyd Garrison began publishing an antislavery newspaper, *The Liberator*, on January 1, 1831. He also helped form the American Anti-Slavery Society, which tried to coordinate the activities of many local abolitionist societies. In all, about 200,000 people joined the organization.

Although slavery was legal, Garrison felt it was wrong. "That which is not just is not law," he wrote.

The radical tone of *The Liberator* was different from previous abolitionist publications because it labeled slave owners as criminals and called for immediate abolition. Some abolitionists, like John Brown, believed violence was the only way to end slavery.

The actions of the more militant abolitionists brought the issue of slavery to national attention and were another factor contributing to the outbreak of the Civil War.

1. What is your opinion of the plan to free slaves and return them to Africa?

   _____

   _____

   _____

2. Do you agree or disagree with Garrison on his statement about the law? Why?

   _____

   _____

   _____

3. If you had lived in the 1800s, what would you have done about slavery?

   _____

   _____

   _____

4. If you'd had the chance, how would you have convinced a slave owner to free his slaves?

   _____

   _____

   _____

   _____

Name:_____ Date:_____

Meet Nat Turner

From the time he was very young, Nat Turner's mother and other slaves believed he was a prophet with mysterious powers. A popular religious leader and a powerful preacher, Nat strongly believed his purpose in life was to free the slaves. He claimed he heard voices and had visions.

On August 21, 1831, he and five slaves killed their master and his family. They were joined by approximately 60 other slaves from nearby plantations. Nat led the band of slaves against White slave owners, killing more than 50 White men, women, and children.

The group planned to attack the county seat at Jerusalem, Virginia, to obtain supplies and money. However, White militiamen and volunteers attacked and ended the revolt on August 24.

Although many of Nat's men were captured and hanged, Nat escaped to the Great Dismal Swamp where a large group of fugitives lived. There he hid out for several weeks.

Born a slave in Southhampton County, Virginia, in 1800, Nat Turner led a rebellion in 1831 that had disastrous consequences.

Most of Turner's followers were eventually captured, but the hunt for Turner himself went on. Slaves were roughly questioned and their quarters searched.

Finally, Nat surrendered. While a prisoner, he stated: "I had a vision and I saw white spirits and black spirits engaged in battle, and the sun was darkened—the thunder rolled in the heavens, and blood flowed in streams. And I heard a voice saying, 'Such is your luck, such you are called to see; and let it come rough or smooth, you must surely bear it.'"

Nat and others who rebelled were tried in November 1831, convicted, and hanged.

1. Consider both sides of the Nat Turner Rebellion. List three reasons why you think Nat Turner was right to lead a rebellion and three reasons why you think he was wrong.

_____

_____

_____

_____

_____

_____

_____

Name:_____ Date:_____

The Effects of Turner's Rebellion

As a result of Nat Turner's rebellion, the Virginia legislature debated whether to end slavery, but the movement to abolish slavery, which had gained some support in the South, was almost completely abandoned.

Rather than freeing any slaves, Nat Turner's actions had the opposite effect. In retaliation, Whites sought revenge, killing 120 Blacks in one day. Most of those were innocent victims who had nothing to do with Turner's rebellion.

Southern legislatures passed stricter controls on slaves. Because Nat Turner could read and write, some slave owners believed that slaves who could read and write were more likely to rebel or run away. Charleston, South Carolina, passed a law forbidding any education for Blacks, whether free or slave.

After Turner's rebellion, slaves were forbidden to have any reading materials, even a Bible. They also enforced stricter controls on Black preachers, fearing that, like Nat Turner, they would have too much influence on slaves.

Free Blacks were not allowed to enter the slave states of Tennessee or Virginia.

It was against the law in North Carolina, Mississippi, and Virginia to distribute any anti-slavery literature. Some Southern states made it a crime to circulate copies of William Lloyd Garrison's abolitionist newspaper, *The Liberator*, and called for prosecution of Garrison.

In response to actions and stricter controls by Whites, more slave revolts occurred in Delaware, Alabama, Kentucky, and Tennessee.

1. How do you think Nat Turner would have felt about innocent Blacks being killed after the rebellion?

   _____

   _____

   _____

2. Why do you think laws were made forbidding freed Blacks from entering Tennessee or Virginia?

   _____

   _____

   _____

3. Many who believed strongly in abolition felt that violence was the only way to reach their goal of freeing all slaves. Do you agree or disagree? On your own paper, explain your answer.

20

Name:_____ Date:_____

Meet John Brown

Born in Connecticut in 1800, John Brown moved with his family to Ohio when he was five. From his father, an active abolitionist, John learned to hate the institution of slavery.

While living in Pennsylvania in 1834, John and other abolitionists began a project to educate Black children. In 1855 he joined five of his sons in Kansas Territory in the fight between those who wanted Kansas to be a slave state and those who wanted Kansas to enter the Union as a free state. Throughout his life he worked for the abolition of slavery.

With financial support from other abolitionists, John began a plan in 1857 to free slaves using a small army. He recruited supporters and established a refuge for fugitive slaves in the mountains of Virginia.

John Brown finally launched his venture on October 16, 1859, with a force of 18 men, including three of his sons. They seized the U.S. arsenal at Harpers Ferry, Virginia, and won control of the town.

John Brown's attempt to end slavery by force at Harpers Ferry increased the tension between the North and South and was another factor contributing to the Civil War.

They retained control for only a short time, however. In a battle with troops led by Colonel Robert E. Lee, many of Brown's followers and two of his sons were killed. John was wounded and forced to surrender. He was arrested and charged with various crimes, including treason and murder. After being found guilty, John Brown was hanged in Charlestown, Virginia, in December 1859.

For many years, John Brown was regarded by abolitionists as a martyr to the cause of human freedom.

1. Use a dictionary. What is an arsenal? _____

_____

_____

2. Use a dictionary. What is treason? _____

_____

_____

3. Why do you think John Brown was charged with treason? _____

_____

_____

_____

_____

Name:_____ Date:_____

The Underground Railroad

The Underground Railroad included a series of houses, caves, hay mounds, root cellars, attics, chimneys, hidden rooms, sheds, and barns—places where runaway slaves could hide for a short time. The Underground Railroad also referred to the paths and trails that led from one shelter to the next and to the people, White and Black, who helped lead slaves to freedom.

Some slaves escaped from the South undetected in a wagon with a false bottom.

Most of the first guides (later called conductors) on the Underground Railroad were slaves or former slaves. Some secretly helped others to freedom but remained slaves. Others were freed slaves who put themselves in danger of becoming imprisoned, killed, or enslaved again by helping runaways. Some were slaves who had fled to freedom and then returned to help friends and family members escape.

Along the route to freedom, runaways stayed in safe houses and secret hiding places called "stations" and "depots" where they could eat and rest before continuing on their journey.

Many of the first Whites who became part of the Underground Railroad were Quakers—members of a religious group who strongly opposed slavery. Other abolitionists in both the North and South helped slaves escape. Although the Fugitive Slave Law of 1850 made it illegal to help runaway slaves, many people ignored the law.

Slave owners feared two things: a major slave uprising and the escape of their slaves. Since a slave could be worth several hundred or even several thousand dollars, a slave who ran away meant an economic loss. They also knew that each slave who escaped encouraged others to try.

1. Since the Underground Railroad was neither underground nor part of a railroad, why do you think this term was used?

   _____

   _____

   _____

2. Why do you think those who led others to freedom were called conductors?

   _____

   _____

3. Do you think it was right or wrong to break the law in order to help runaway slaves? Why?

   _____

   _____

   _____

Name:_____ Date:_____

Conductors on the Underground Railroad

Men and women, both Black and White, became conductors and "station masters" on the Underground Railroad. For Blacks, the danger of returning to the South to help others escape was extremely great. If they were free men or women, they could be sold into slavery if caught. If they were runaways, they could be whipped, beaten, and returned to their masters. When caught, runaways were often sold to masters in the "deep South" where they would have little chance to escape.

A light in the window of a "station" on the Underground Railroad was always a welcome sight to the weary travelers.

Since it was a secret organization, no one knows for sure how many people became part of the Underground Railroad. John Mason, Josiah Henson, J.W. Loguen, John Parker, and Harriet Tubman were among the more than 500 Black conductors on the Underground Railroad.

John Parker lived in Ohio. At night he rowed across the Ohio River to meet runaways and take them to Ohio. Harriet Tubman made 19 trips and led over 300 slaves to freedom.

Thomas Garrett was one of the many abolitionists who became conductors on the Underground Railroad. He provided food and shelter to about 2,500 runaways. Finally he was arrested for breaking the Fugitive Slave Law in 1848. The fine was so heavy he was forced to sell everything he owned to pay it. In spite of that, he stated, "Friend, I haven't a dollar in the world, but if thee knows a fugitive anywhere on the face of the earth who needs a breakfast, send him to me."

Another abolitionist, Levi Coffin, along with his wife Katie, began helping runaways when he lived in South Carolina. After moving to Newport, Indiana, in 1826, his home became a station on the Underground Railroad. A hundred runaways stopped at his station each year on their way to freedom in Canada.

1. List words that describe the action of men and women who were conductors on the Underground Railroad.

_____

_____

_____

2. On your own paper, write a short poem or song about the Underground Railroad. (For a song, feel free to use a familiar tune and write new words.)

23

Name:_____ Date: _____

Meet Harriet Ross Tubman

One of 11 children, Harriet Tubman was born a slave on a Maryland plantation about 1820. She began working when she was six years old and never attended school. Harriet worked as a house servant and in the fields.

When she was 11, Harriet refused to help hold a slave while his owner punished him for trying to escape. The overseer threw a heavy iron weight at the runaway, but it missed and hit Harriet. As a result, she had dizziness and fainting spells for the rest of her life.

In 1844 Harriet married a free Black man, John Tubman, but she remained a slave. When Harriet learned that her master planned to sell her, she decided to run away. Although she was scared, Harriet continued on the Underground Railroad to Pennsylvania where slavery was illegal.

Slaves called her Moses, because like Moses in the Bible, Harriet Tubman led her people from slavery to freedom.

After she was free, Harriet returned secretly to Maryland to rescue family members and many other slaves, leading them all to safety. Harriet later said, "On my Underground Railroad I never ran my train off the track, and I never lost a passenger."

John Tubman refused to join his wife, and he later remarried. Harriet made at least 19 trips, rescuing over 300 slaves, including her parents who were over 70 years old at the time.

Southern plantation owners offered a $40,000 reward for her capture, dead or alive.

During the Civil War, Harriet served the Union Army as a cook, nurse, spy, and scout, but she was never paid for her work. After the war, Harriet married Nelson Davis and bought a home in Auburn, New York.

Harriet helped organize the National Federation of Afro-American Women, opened a home for the aged, assisted the sick and hungry, and helped set up schools for freed slaves. She died on March 10, 1913.

1. Use what you learned about Harriet Tubman to write a test for a partner on your own paper. Write 10 questions. They can be true and false, matching, or fill in the blanks. Trade papers with a partner and take each other's test.

2. Harriet Tubman was called "the Moses of her people." Why was this an appropriate name for her?

_____

_____

Name:_____   Date:_____

The Missouri Compromise

Henry Clay

The Northwest Ordinance of 1787 prohibited slavery in all American territories north and west of the Ohio River. When Missouri applied for statehood in 1819 as a slave state (a state where slavery was legal), many Northerners objected. At that time there were 11 free states and 11 slave states. By adding another slave state, the balance of power in the Senate would go to those who were for slavery.

The debate in Congress was long and bitter. Most Northern congressmen refused to accept Missouri as a slave state. They wanted to completely stop the spread of slavery forever, even if they couldn't eliminate it in the South.

Southern congressmen felt that since the Constitution granted the right to own slaves, that right would be taken away if Missouri became a free state, because all slave owners in Missouri would lose their slaves. They felt it was the duty of the federal government to protect private property.

1. Do you agree or disagree with this argument? Explain your reasons on your own paper.

At that time, Maine was not a separate state; it was part of Massachusetts. Maine also applied for statehood. Southern congressmen refused to allow Maine to enter the Union as a free state unless Missouri was allowed to enter as a slave state.

Then Henry Clay created the Missouri Compromise, which was passed by Congress in 1820. Henry Clay was a nationally respected political figure whose genius was in finding a political middle ground when compromise seemed impossible. The Compromise allowed Missouri to become a slave state and Maine to enter as a free state. In addition, a line was drawn through the Louisiana Purchase at the southern border of Missouri. North of that line, slavery was prohibited forever.

Many Northerners were unhappy with the compromise because it allowed another state to make slavery legal. Many Southerners were unhappy because they felt they had the right to take their property anywhere in the United States. Although the Missouri Compromise became a law in 1820, few people on either side of the slavery issue were happy about it.

2. Why do you think Southern Congressmen didn't want Maine to enter as a free state?

    _____

    _____

3. Would you have voted for the Missouri Compromise? Why or why not?

    _____

    _____

Name:_____ Date:_____

The Kansas-Nebraska Act

Slavery became a major issue again when the Nebraska Territory was opened up for settlement. At that time, the area included the modern states of Kansas, Nebraska, and parts of North and South Dakota, Montana, Wyoming, Idaho, and Colorado.

In 1854 Congress passed the Kansas-Nebraska Act, which repealed the section of the Missouri Compromise that banned more slave states north of a line drawn through the Louisiana Purchase at the southern border of Missouri.

One reason for this change was because of the addition of more territory in the Southwest after the Mexican War. This included California, Texas, Nevada, Utah, New Mexico, Arizona, and parts of Idaho, Wyoming, and Colorado.

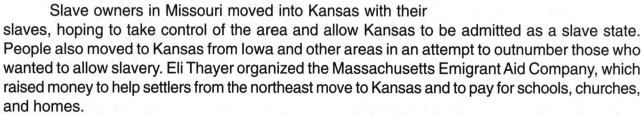

The Kansas-Nebraska Act allowed inhabitants of each territory to decide for themselves whether they wanted to apply for statehood as a free state or a slave state.

Slave owners in Missouri moved into Kansas with their slaves, hoping to take control of the area and allow Kansas to be admitted as a slave state. People also moved to Kansas from Iowa and other areas in an attempt to outnumber those who wanted to allow slavery. Eli Thayer organized the Massachusetts Emigrant Aid Company, which raised money to help settlers from the northeast move to Kansas and to pay for schools, churches, and homes.

Violent battles occurred between proslavery settlers and antislavery settlers. The battles turned into a bloody war. Kansas was known for a time as "Bleeding Kansas." Fighting continued for several years, extending the hard feelings that eventually led to the Civil War.

1. How do you think abolitionists felt about the Kansas-Nebraska Act?

   _____

   _____

   _____

2. How do you think slave owners felt about the Kansas-Nebraska Act?

   _____

   _____

   _____

3. Use reference sources. When did Kansas become a state? _____

4. Was it a free state or a slave state? _____

Name:_____ Date:_____

The *Dred Scott* Decision

Dred Scott

Dred Scott was born a slave in Virginia about 1800. His owner, Peter Blow, moved to St. Louis in 1830 and sold Dred to John Emerson, an army surgeon. When Emerson went to Illinois, then to Fort Snelling, an army post in the Wisconsin Territory, he took his slave with him.

While at Fort Snelling, Dred Scott married another slave, Harriet Robinson. The Scotts remained at Fort Snelling after Emerson returned to St. Louis and then joined him in 1840.

After Emerson died, Dred Scott went to court to obtain freedom for himself, his wife, and their two daughters. He claimed that because they had lived in a free state and a free territory, they had been free, even though they had returned to a slave state. Once free, they should remain free.

The St. Louis Circuit Court agreed, but the Missouri Supreme Court reversed the decision, claiming that Missouri would not recognize any federal or state laws that freed slaves. Therefore, the Scotts were slaves and always had been.

Dred Scott appealed to the U.S. Supreme Court. In a 7 to 2 decision in 1857, the court decided that Dred Scott was a slave, not a citizen, and therefore not entitled to sue in a federal court. Chief Justice Taney also claimed that even free Blacks were not and could never be U.S. citizens. (Even though free Black men were considered citizens and allowed to vote in several Northern states.)

Although the case took several years before a decision was made, both those who were proslavery and those who were against it were very interested in hearing the outcome.

Shortly after the Supreme Court decision, the son of Dred Scott's first owner purchased him and his family and set them free.

Although the Dred Scott case had nothing to do with the Missouri Compromise, Chief Justice Taney also declared that the portion of the Missouri Compromise banning slavery north and west of Missouri was unconstitutional, because Congress did not have the power to prohibit slavery in federal territories.

1. What decision do you think slave owners wanted the Supreme Court to reach? Why?

   _____

   _____

   _____

2. What decision do you think abolitionists wanted the Supreme Court to reach? Why?

   _____

   _____

   _____

Name:_____ Date: _____

Similes and Metaphors

A **simile** is a figure of speech that uses *like* or *as* to compare two things that are not alike.

Example: Slave owners believed slaves were like other forms of property.

A **metaphor** is a figure of speech that uses a noun or noun phrase to make a direct comparison between two unlike things. The words *like* or *as* are not used in a metaphor.

Example: Slaves were considered property.

Write "M" for metaphor or "S" for simile on the line before each sentence.

_____ 1. Freedom was a shining star.

_____ 2. Freedom seemed as far away as the moon.

_____ 3. The Underground Railroad was a road to freedom.

_____ 4. Harriet Tubman was like Moses: she led her people to freedom.

_____ 5. Slaves were packed like sardines on slave ships.

Finish the similes.

6. The slave was treated like _____.

7. The idea of freedom was like _____.

8. He shook like _____ when he heard the slave hunter's hounds.

9. She was as frightened as _____ when she was sold to a new master.

Finish the metaphors.

10. His life as a slave was _____.

11. Their dream of freedom was _____.

12. The slaves' songs were _____.

Write two similes.

13. _____

14. _____

Write two metaphors.

15. _____

16. _____

Name:_____ Date:_____

What Would You Do?

1. You have been asked to hide a runaway slave overnight. If you get caught, you will be sent to prison. What would you do?

   _____

   _____

   _____

2. The publisher of an antislavery newspaper has asked you to write an article for his newspaper. Many of the reporters for this newspaper have been attacked by angry mobs, beaten, and their homes burned. What would you do?

   _____

   _____

   _____

3. You have learned about secret plans for a slave rebellion. You believe slavery is wrong, but you know that many innocent people may be killed in the rebellion. What would you do?

   _____

   _____

   _____

4. Your parents are slave owners on a Southern plantation. They treat their slaves fairly well. You discover that a Black woman who has taken care of you since you were a baby is planning to run away. You will miss her very much, and you know her chances of escape are not very good. What would you do?

   _____

   _____

   _____

5. You are Abraham Lincoln. A time traveler has told you that if you run for president, you will win, but the Civil War will begin, thousands will die in the war, and you will be assassinated. What would you do?

   _____

   _____

   _____

Name: _____   Date: _____

Meet Sojourner Truth

Named Isabella by her parents, she changed her name to Sojourner Truth in 1843. Sojourner was sold several times to different masters. When New York passed a law freeing all slaves in the state, her master refused to free her. She ran away to New York City where she found a job as a maid.

Sojourner heard voices she believed to be from God. She began preaching in New York City in 1829. Later she made a lecture tour through Massachusetts, Connecticut, Ohio, Indiana, Illinois, and Kansas.

"I went to the Lord and asked him to give me a new name. And the Lord gave me Sojourner because I was to travel up and down the land showing the people their sins and being a sign unto them. Afterwards, I told the Lord I wanted another name

Born a slave in New York about 1797, Sojourner Truth became one of the leading abolitionists as well as an advocate of women's rights.

'cause everybody else had two names; and the Lord gave me Truth, because I was to declare the truth to the people."

Sojourner preached and spoke in favor of the abolitionist movement, becoming the most famous antislavery speaker of the time. Although illiterate, she was a very effective speaker, and large crowds gathered to listen.

Sojourner was not active in the Underground Railroad, but she inspired many to travel that path to freedom. Attempts were made to stop her from speaking out.

Besides freedom for slaves, she advocated women's rights and a Negro State in the west on public lands.

1. Use a dictionary. What does *sojourner* mean? _____

   _____

2. Use a dictionary. What does *illiterate* mean? _____

   _____

3. Do you think a Negro State in the West would have been a good idea? Why or why not?

   _____

   _____

   _____

   _____

   _____

   _____

Name:_____ Date:_____

Interview a Slave

You are a reporter for an abolitionist newspaper. Your assignment is to interview a slave for an article against slavery.

What is the name and age of the person you will interview?

_____

Write twelve questions you might ask that person during an interview.

1. _____

_____

2. _____

_____

3. _____

_____

4. _____

_____

5. _____

_____

6. _____

_____

7. _____

_____

8. _____

_____

9. _____

_____

10. _____

_____

11. _____

_____

12. _____

_____

Name:_____ Date:_____

Write All About It

The year is 1860. You work for an abolitionist newspaper and have strong feelings about the evils of slavery and the rights of all people to "life, liberty, and the pursuit of happiness." Some people believe violence is the only way to end slavery. Others have suggested that the country be divided into two separate nations.

What do you think should be done? Write an opinion essay for your newspaper to convince others to see your point of view.

_____

_____

_____

_____

_____

_____

_____

_____

_____

_____

_____

_____

_____

_____

_____

_____

_____

Name:_____ Date:_____

Interview a Slave Owner

You are a reporter for a Southern newspaper. Your assignment is to interview a slave owner for an article about why slavery should be allowed.

What is the name and age of the person you will interview?

_____

Write twelve questions you might ask that person during an interview.

1. _____
   _____

2. _____
   _____

3. _____
   _____

4. _____
   _____

5. _____
   _____

6. _____
   _____

7. _____
   _____

8. _____
   _____

9. _____
   _____

10. _____
    _____

11. _____
    _____

12. _____
    _____

Name:_____ Date:_____

Meet Frederick Douglass

Frederick Douglass was born a slave about 1817. His owner's wife began teaching him to read and write—until her husband found out. Hugh Auld, like many other slave owners, believed it was more likely for educated slaves to try to escape.

When Hugh Auld died, Frederick went to work as a field hand on Thomas Auld's plantation where slaves were starved, beaten, and forced to work very hard.

When he was 15, Frederick helped organize a Sunday school for slaves that was shut down by angry Whites. His master decided Frederick was a troublemaker and sent him to a "slave breaker"—a person who beat disobedient slaves until they were less rebellious. After many beatings, Frederick fought back, and the slave breaker sent him back to his master.

Following an unsuccessful escape, Auld sent Frederick to Baltimore to work in the shipyards. His wages were given to his master.

Disguised as a sailor, Frederick escaped to New York where he married Anna Murray, a free Black woman. They moved to New Bedford, Massachusetts.

Invited to talk about his experiences as a slave by the American Anti-Slavery Society, Frederick discovered his true talent as a speaker and leader in the crusade for freedom.

Frederick published *Narrative of the Life of Frederick Douglass, an American Slave*, although friends feared he would be recognized as a runaway slave and recaptured. The book was well-read in the North and Europe. Following a two-year lecture tour in England, Frederick raised enough money to buy his freedom.

Frederick Douglass published an antislavery newspaper, *The North Star.* His home in Rochester, New York, became a station on the Underground Railroad.

1. Why do you think slave owners believed knowing how to read and write would cause slaves to try to escape?

   _____

   _____

   _____

2. Use a dictionary. What does *crusade* mean? _____

   _____

3. Why do you think Frederick Douglass published his book? _____

   _____

   _____

Name:_____ Date: _____

Journal of a Slave

Imagine being a slave working in the fields on a Southern plantation. Your master is cruel. You are forced to work hard and are fed very little. You dream of freedom. Write four journal entries for the dates given. Continue the entries on your own paper if you need more space.

December 24, 1851: (Describe your life on the plantation.)

_____

_____

_____

_____

_____

February 28, 1852: (Explain why you are planning to run away.)

_____

_____

_____

_____

_____

July 4, 1852: (Describe your escape plan.)

_____

_____

_____

_____

October 31, 1852: (Describe your escape attempt and where you are now.)

_____

_____

_____

_____

_____

Name:_____ Date: _____

Tidbits of Historical Trivia

- The first public slave auction in North America was held in Jamestown in 1638.

- Historians estimate that in the late 1600s, about one of every four slaves died while crossing the Atlantic Ocean.

- According to Dr. Samuel Cartwright, slaves who ran away were infected with drapetomania, the "running-away disease." He believed slaves who deliberately broke tools to avoid work suffered from "Dysthesia Aethiopiea, or Herbitude of the Mind and Obtuse Sensibility of Body." His cure for both diseases was severe whipping.

- Liberia was founded on the West Coast of Africa in 1822 by the American Colonization Society as a refuge for freed slaves. Named in honor of President James Monroe, many former slaves resettled in the colony of Monrovia in the nineteenth century.

- Frederick Douglass was forced to flee to Canada when Virginia issued an arrest warrant charging him with conspiring with John Brown in the raid on Harpers Ferry. Douglass had met Brown and advised him to give up his plan.

- Henry Brown found a unique way to escape slavery. He had a carpenter build a wooden crate, and he hid inside it. The crate was shipped from Richmond, Virginia, to abolitionists in Philadelphia.

- Thomas Jefferson introduced a bill barring slavery from all future states admitted to the Union, but it was defeated in Congress by one vote.

- At their yearly meeting in 1696, the American Quakers agreed to ban importation of slaves. If a member violated this ban, he or she would be expelled from the group.

- In 1857, George Fitzhugh of Virginia published a book, *Slaves Without Masters*. He claimed that slaves were treated better than factory workers in the North because factory workers had no guarantee of support when they were ill or too old to work.

1. Use reference sources to find two other interesting bits of historical trivia.

_____

_____

_____

_____

Name:_____ Date:_____

Meet Harriet Beecher Stowe

Harriet Beecher Stowe

Harriet Beecher was born on June 14, 1811, in Litchfield, Connecticut. She and her seven brothers and sisters grew up in New England. Their mother died when Harriet was five, so the children were raised by an aunt and a stepmother. Harriet attended the Hartford Female Seminary, a school run by her sister, Catherine; she later became a teacher there. When her father, a minister, moved to Cincinnati, Ohio, in 1832, Harriet and her sister moved with him. Catherine started another girls' school, and Harriet continued to teach.

Although slavery was not allowed in Ohio, it was legal across the Ohio River in Kentucky. Here Harriet and her family were first exposed to the realities of slavery. They talked to former slaves and fugitives and heard stories of cruelty and the separation of husbands from wives and parents from children. They read advertisements for the return of runaway slaves and saw slave catchers on the streets.

Harriet married Reverend Calvin Stowe in 1836. Their son Charley died of cholera in 1849.

When a Black woman hired by the Stowes confessed she was a runaway slave, Harriet and her husband helped her escape to Canada. Harriet visited the home of a student, a slave plantation in Kentucky, where she saw slavery firsthand.

When her husband was offered a position at Bowdoin College in Brunswick, Maine, Harriet was glad to leave Cincinnati.

After moving to Maine, Harriet gave birth to her sixth child. The family had little money. Although she had a new baby, four other children, and a home to care for, Harriet helped support her family by writing newspaper and magazine articles. She published her first book, *The Mayflower, or Sketches of Scenes and Characters Among the Descendants of the Pilgrims* in 1843.

1. Imagine being the daughter of a minister who grew up in New England in the early 1800s. How would you have felt about what you saw and heard in Ohio and Kentucky?

_____

_____

_____

_____

_____

Name: _____ Date: _____

Uncle Tom's Cabin

When Congress passed the Fugitive Slave Act of 1850, Harriet Beecher Stowe's sister wrote her: "If I could use a pen as you can, I would write something that will make this nation feel what an accursed thing slavery is."

Harriet decided to write a fictional story about slavery as a serial for an antislavery magazine called the *National Era*. The story, published in 1851 and 1852, grew as she painted a vivid picture of what she had seen and heard about slavery. She wove her story around fictional characters and situations based on real people and experiences.

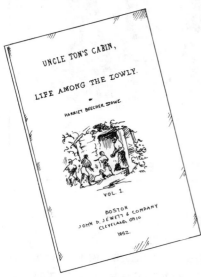

Soon after the serial was complete, it was published as a book.

Harriet hoped to earn a little money from the book to help out her family. The first 5,000 copies sold out in two days. Another 20,000 copies sold in the next three weeks. The publisher couldn't keep up with the demand for copies. The book was also published in Great Britain and translated into other languages. Although the book was banned in the South, it sold over 500,000 copies in the first five years.

Although it was far from great literature, Harriet's book helped readers see slaves as real people in an unjust and cruel situation. *Uncle Tom's Cabin* drew so much attention and was read by so many people, it may have been one factor that led to the Civil War.

1. Use a dictionary. Define *serial*. _____

   _____

2. Why do you think *Uncle Tom's Cabin* was popular in the North?

   _____

   _____

   _____

3. Why do you think Harriet's book was popular in England and foreign countries?

   _____

   _____

   _____

4. Why do you think her book was banned in the South?

   _____

   _____

   _____

Name:_____ Date:_____

Fact or Opinion?

A **fact** is a statement that can be verified as true.

> **Fact:** Thousands of Africans were forced into slavery.

An **opinion** is a statement that cannot be verified as true.

> **Opinion:** Harriet Beecher Stowe was a good writer.

Write "F" for fact or "O" for opinion on the line by each statement.

_____ 1. Sojourner Truth lectured to many people about the evils of slavery.

_____ 2. Nat Turner led a slave rebellion in 1831.

_____ 3. Nat Turner was wrong to lead a rebellion.

_____ 4. Nat Turner was right to lead a rebellion.

_____ 5. Abraham Lincoln issued the Emancipation Proclamation.

_____ 6. Abraham Lincoln was the best U.S. President.

_____ 7. Harriet Beecher Stowe's novel, *Uncle Tom's Cabin,* was very popular, especially in the North.

_____ 8. George Washington and Thomas Jefferson were both slave owners.

_____ 9. If slave owners would have treated their slaves well, no one would have complained.

_____ 10. All conductors on the Underground Railroad were very brave.

11. Write two facts about slavery.

_____

_____

12. Write two opinions about slavery.

_____

_____

Name:_____ Date:_____

Spirituals

Slaves sang as they worked, when they gathered together in the evening, as they rejoiced, and when they were sad. Among the most prominent songs sung by slaves were the spirituals.

Spirituals came from the time of slavery, and their creation ended when slavery ended. The names of those who wrote the words are lost. Some of the melodies were original. Some were derived from older songs, American, African, and a combination of both. Nearly 1,000 examples of spirituals have been collected. They are unique in the song literature of the world. It is ironic that one of America's most distinctive contributions to world music is derived from the time when slavery was legal in the United States.

Some spirituals have a religious tone. Many are about the pain and suffering endured by the slaves. Some spirituals speak with longing of a "promised land"—a land where slaves are free.

Use the Internet or other reference sources. Read the words to one of the songs listed. Describe the mood of the song. On another sheet of paper, explain what the words mean.

Almost Over	Hold Out to the End	O Daniel
Away Down in Sunbury	I Can't Stay Behind	O Don't Feel Weary
Blow Your Trumpet, Gabriel	I'm Going Home	Old Ship of Zion
Bound to Go	I'm in Trouble	O Shout Away
Brother, Guide Me Home	In the Mansions Above	Poor Rosy
Brother Moses Gone	I Want to Go Home	Pray On
Build a House in Paradise	Jacob's Ladder	Religion So Sweet
Come Go With Me	Join the Angel Band	Rock O' My Soul
Don't be Weary, Traveler	Jordan's Mills	Roll, Jordan, Roll
Early in the Morning	Just Now	Shall I Die?
Every Hour in the Day	Lay This Body Down	Shout On, Children
Fare Ye Well	Lonesome Valley	Stars Begin to Fall
Give up the World	Lord, Remember Me	Travel On
God Got Plenty of Room	Many Thousand Go	Wake Up, Jacob
Go In the Wilderness	Meet, O Lord	What a Trying Time
Good-Bye	Michael, Row the Boat Ashore	We Will March Through the
The Graveyard	My Father, How Long?	Valley
Hallelu, Hallelu	Nobody Knows the Trouble	Winter
Happy Morning	I've Seen	
Heave Away	Not Weary Yet	

Name:_____ Date:_____

Haiku of Freedom

Haiku poetry is often written about nature or about subjects for which the writer has strong feelings. Haiku poems follow a specific pattern:

Line 1 = 5 syllables
Line 2 = 7 syllables
Line 3 = 5 syllables

Sample: Life and Liberty,
                   The pursuit of happiness
                   When will I be free?

Write a title for the sample poem. _____

Imagine being a slave who is mistreated and dreams of freedom. Write a haiku expressing your feelings.

Prewrite: List words you might use in your poem. _____

_____

Write your rough draft. In a short poem like this, every word is important. Polish your poem until it fits the haiku pattern.

_____

_____

_____

_____

Write a title for your poem. _____

When you finish, write the final version.

_____

_____

_____

_____

Name:_____   Date:_____

Get to Know Someone

1. Read a biography or autobiography of a person who was once a slave. A list of possible titles can be found on page 60.

2. Fill in the blanks with information from the book.

    Book title: _____

    Person's name: _____

    Date of birth (if known): _____

    Place of birth (if known): _____

    Date of death: _____

3. Do a character sketch by filling in the chart below. Write a word in the first column that describes the main character. Then, in the second column, briefly describe a specific incident from the book that illustrates how that word applies to the person you read about.

    Example: *Brave:* She was brave when she prevented her master from beating her sister.

Descriptive Word	Specific Example

Name:_____ Date:_____

Alike and Different

Use the Internet or other reference sources to learn more about any two of the people listed. Use the Venn diagram to do a comparison.

John Brown
William Lloyd Garrison
Harriet Beecher Stowe
Sojourner Truth
Dred Scott

Frederick Douglass
Abraham Lincoln
Nat Turner
Harriet Ross Tubman
Phillis Wheatley

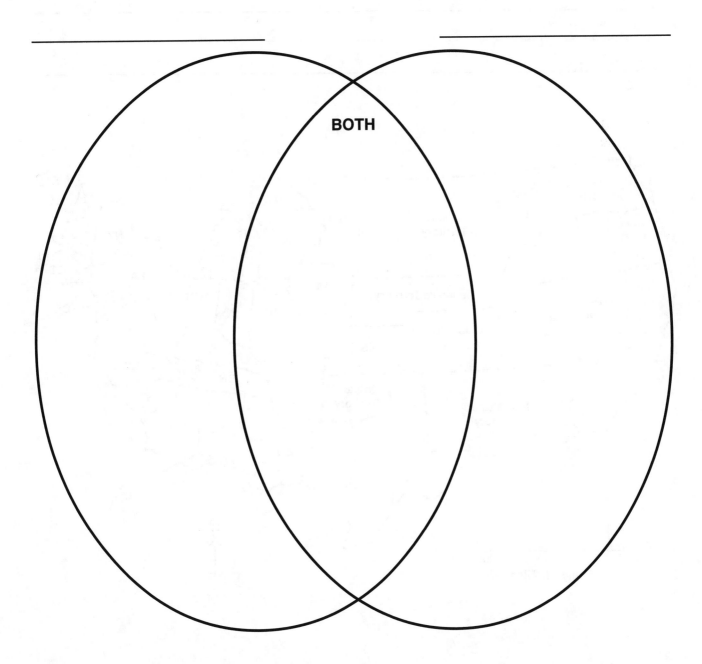

BOTH

Name:_____ Date:_____

The Union Is Divided

In 1861 Alabama, Arkansas, Florida, Georgia, Louisiana, Mississippi, North Carolina, South Carolina, Tennessee, Texas, and Virginia seceded from the Union.

1. Color these states grey.

2. Color the states blue that did not secede.

3. The section called Indian Territory later became what state? _____

4. Name the other seven U.S. territories shown on the map. _____

_____

_____

_____

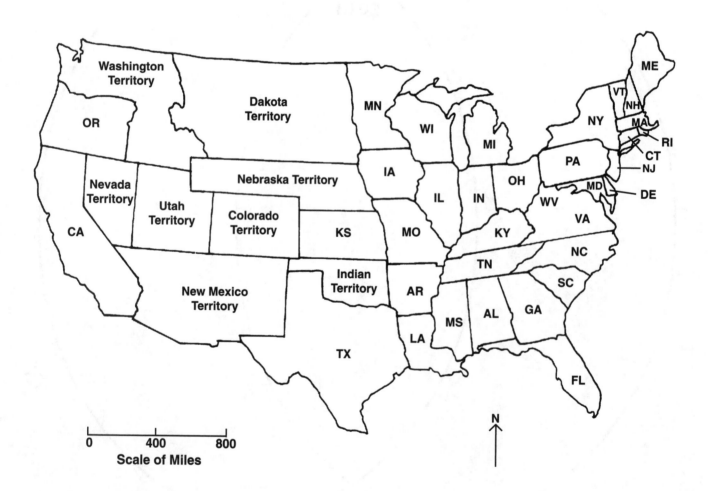

Name:_____ Date:_____

Lincoln's Views on Slavery

Abraham Lincoln, the sixteenth President of the United States, is best known for his famous Gettysburg Address, a speech he gave at the Gettysburg battlefield during the Civil War. In the Gettysburg Address he began by saying:

"Four score and seven years ago, our fathers brought forth on this continent, a new nation, conceived in Liberty, and dedicated to the proposition that all men are created equal."

On many occasions, Lincoln clearly stated his belief that slavery was wrong and that all men were created equal.

Read the words of Abraham Lincoln below. Under his words, write your opinion of what he said. Explain what you think he meant, if you agree or not, and why. Use your own paper if you need more room.

1. During the debate about whether Kansas should be a free state or a slave state, Lincoln said:

"It is said that the slave holder has the same political right to take his Negroes to Kansas that a freeman has to take his hogs or his horses. This would be true if Negroes were property in the same sense that hogs and horses are. But is this the case? It is notoriously not so."

_____

_____

_____

_____

_____

2. Lincoln was referring to the Declaration of Independence, which states that "... all Men are created equal ...," when he spoke these words:

"Let us discard all this quibbling about this man and that man—this race and the other race, being inferior, and therefore they must be placed in an inferior position. Let us discard all these things, and unite as one people throughout the land, until we shall once more stand up declaring that all men are created equal."

_____

_____

_____

_____

Name:_____   Date: _____

Jefferson Davis or Abraham Lincoln?

During the Civil War, Abraham Lincoln and Jefferson Davis were prominent leaders. Abraham Lincoln was President of the United States of America. Jefferson Davis was President of the Confederate States of America.

Use the Internet and other reference sources. Write "AL" on the blank if the statement refers to Abraham Lincoln. Write "JD" if it refers to Jefferson Davis. Write BOTH if the statement refers to both men.

Jefferson Davis

_____ 1. He was born in 1808.

_____ 2. He was born in Kentucky.

_____ 3. He was a lawyer.

_____ 4. He married Mary Todd.

_____ 5. He had four sons; three of them died before becoming adults.

_____ 6. He served as Secretary of War when Franklin Pierce was president.

_____ 7. He attended Transylvania University.

_____ 8. He served in the U.S. Congress.

_____ 9. His father, Thomas, was a carpenter.

_____ 10. He attended West Point Military Academy.

_____ 11. He was appointed postmaster of New Salem and worked as the deputy surveyor of Sangamon County.

_____ 12. His wife died three months after they were married.

Abraham Lincoln

_____ 13. His career included terms in both the House and the Senate.

_____ 14. Many citizens accused him of not doing everything possible to end the war.

_____ 15. He did not care to be president; he would have much preferred being a general.

Name:_____   Date:_____

The Emancipation Proclamation

The Emancipation Proclamation issued by Abraham Lincoln declared that as of January 1, 1863, all slaves in all states or parts of states that were in rebellion against the United States shall be free.

1. Did the Emancipation Proclamation free all slaves? _____

The Emancipation Proclamation actually freed about one million slaves. It didn't apply to the three million slaves in states that had not seceded from the Union, or even in certain areas of states that had seceded. The states that had formed the Confederacy did not act on Lincoln's order. The Proclamation did show the world that the United States was serious about ending slavery.

In the Emancipation Proclamation, Lincoln declared that the government, army, and navy would recognize and maintain their freedom and would do nothing to stop these slaves "in any efforts they may make for their actual freedom."

2. What do you think that statement means? _____

_____

_____

_____

Lincoln went on to state: "… I hereby enjoin upon the people so declared to be free to abstain from all violence, unless in necessary self-defence; and I recommend to them that, in all cases when allowed, they labor faithfully for reasonable wages."

3. Rewrite the above quote in your own words. _____

_____

_____

_____

_____

_____

The Thirteenth Amendment, passed in 1865, officially abolished slavery in the United States; however, slaves were not considered "citizens" and did not have the right to vote until another amendment was passed.

4. Which amendment to the Constitution gave Black men the right to vote? _____

5. When was that amendment passed? _____

6. Which amendment gave women the right the vote? _____

7. In what year was that amendment passed? _____

Name:_____ Date:_____

Matching Activity

Write words from the word bank to match the definitions.

abolitionists	arsenal	John Brown	compromise
Jefferson Davis	treason	Frederick Douglass	emancipation
Harriet Beecher Stowe	fugitive	Abraham Lincoln	illiterate
inhumane	retribution	Harriet Tubman	sojourner

1. _____ Not able to read or write

2. _____ An agreement between two people or groups in which each gives up something

3. _____ A traveler

4. _____ People who believed slavery was wrong

5. _____ Author of *Uncle Tom's Cabin*

6. _____ Conductor on the Underground Railroad

7. _____ Punishment for doing something wrong

8. _____ A place where weapons and ammunition are stored

9. _____ Betrayal of one's country

10. _____ Freedom from slavery

11. _____ Led a raid on Harpers Ferry

12. _____ Issued the Emancipation Proclamation

13. _____ President of the Confederate States of America

14. _____ A runaway

15. _____ Cruel treatment of other people

16. _____ Author of an autobiography about his life as a slave

Name:_____ Date:_____

Cause and Effect

A **cause** is an event that produces a result. An **effect** is the result produced. For each cause, write a possible effect.

Cause	Effect

Cause   **Effect**

1. Harriet Beecher Stowe
   published *Uncle Tom's Cabin*.   _____
                                           _____
                                           _____

2. The Fugitive Slave Law of
   1850 penalized anyone who   _____
   helped a runaway slave.   _____
                                           _____

3. Millions of Africans were
   captured and sold as slaves.   _____
                                           _____
                                           _____

4. Lincoln issued the
   Emancipation Proclamation.   _____
                                           _____
                                           _____

5. States in the South
   seceded from the Union.   _____
                                           _____
                                           _____

6. The Declaration of Independence   _____
   did not grant freedom to   _____
   African-Americans, Native   _____
   Americans, or women.

7. Elizabeth Freeman went to
   court to obtain her freedom.   _____
                                           _____
                                           _____

8. Dred Scott went to court to   _____
   obtain his freedom.   _____
                                           _____

9. Congress passed the
   Missouri Compromise.   _____
                                           _____
                                           _____

Name:_____ Date: _____

True or False?

Circle "T" for True or "F" for False.

1.   T   F   The United States was the only country where slavery was once legal.

2.   T   F   The Emancipation Proclamation abolished slavery everywhere in the United States.

3.   T   F   Abraham Lincoln was president when the Civil War began.

4.   T   F   Harriet Ross Tubman was nicknamed "Moses."

5.   T   F   The federal government passed Fugitive Slave Laws that allowed slave owners to capture runaways, even in states where slavery was illegal.

6.   T   F   Portugal was the first European country to take people from Africa as slaves.

7.   T   F   Of all the European countries, England participated in the slave trade very little.

8.   T   F   Only Africans and their descendants were ever held as slaves in the New World.

9.   T   F   The first African slaves in what later became the United States were taken to Jamestown.

10.   T   F   The section of the Declaration of Independence abolishing slavery was deleted before the document was signed.

11.   T   F   The escape route used by slaves was called the Underground Railroad because slaves traveled hundreds of miles underground in tunnels from the South to Canada.

12.   T   F   People who helped slaves escape along the Underground Railroad were called engineers.

13.   T   F   Slavery was only legal in the South, never in the northern part of the United States.

14.   T   F   John Brown, a fugitive slave, led a raid on the arsenal at Harpers Ferry.

15.   T   F   *Uncle Tom's Cabin* was first published as a serial in a magazine.

Name:_____ Date:_____

In the News

A newspaper headline is a summary of the most important point in an article. Headlines must be brief, to the point, and grab the reader's attention.

Write headlines in six words or less for each event.

1. The first ship carrying slaves to America landed at the colony of Jamestown in Virginia.

   _____

2. The Fugitive Slave Law of 1850 allowed slave owners to take slaves back to their homes, even if they had escaped to a free state. The law also made it illegal to help a slave escape.

   _____

3. Members of the Constitutional Convention agreed to compromise on the issue of slavery and to count each slave as $\frac{3}{5}$ of a person for representation.

   _____

4. The Declaration of Independence states that "all Men are created equal" but does not grant any rights to African-Americans, Native Americans, or women.

   _____

5. Sojourner Truth, the leading speaker for the abolitionist movement, was assaulted by an angry mob on her way to a meeting. She escaped unharmed with the aid of friends.

   _____

6. John Brown attempted to free slaves by force. He launched a raid on the U.S. arsenal at Harpers Ferry on October 16, 1859, with 18 men, including three of his sons.

   _____

7. Many slaves escaped from their owners in the South by traveling north on the Underground Railroad.

   _____

8. Congress passed the Missouri Compromise allowing Missouri to become a slave state and Maine to become a free state. It also made it illegal for any new slave states to be formed in specific areas.

   _____

Name:_____ Date:_____

Figuratively Speaking

Some commonly used figures of speech say one thing, but actually mean something else.

Example: "**Raining cats and dogs**" means it's raining very hard, not that mammals are falling from the sky.

Explain in your own words what each phrase in bold means.

1. Most slave owners ruled their slaves **with an iron hand**.

   _____

2. When the runaway slave heard the slave catcher's hounds, he feared he had jumped **out of the frying pan and into the fire**.

   _____

3. The founding fathers tried to ignore the issue of slavery by **putting it on the back burner**.

   _____

4. When the slave had a chance to escape, he **made a beeline** for the North.

   _____

5. As soon as she left the plantation, she knew she had **burned her bridges behind her**.

   _____

6. To many slaves, the idea of freedom was like a **castle in the air**.

   _____

7. Slavery was a **double-edged sword**. Slave owners made money from their slaves but feared they would revolt.

   _____

8. Harriet Beecher Stowe's novel, *Uncle Tom's Cabin*, **fanned the flames** of the abolitionist movement.

   _____

Name:_____ Date:_____

Historical Math

1. The colony of Massachusetts legalized slavery in 1641 and did not abolish it until 1783. For how many years was slavery legal in Massachusetts? _____

2. How many years passed between the time the Declaration of Independence was written in 1776 and the U.S. Constitution was written in 1787?

3. Nat Turner was born in 1800. He was convicted of treason in 1831. How old was he at that time? _____

4. Sojourner Truth changed her name from Isabella in 1843. She died in 1883. How many years was she known by her new name? _____

5. For purposes of representation, one slave was counted as $\frac{3}{5}$ of a person. How many slaves would it take to equal 12 White people? _____

6. If there were one million slaves in a state, how many "people" would be counted? (Hint: multiply $\frac{3}{5}$ x 1,000,000.) _____

7. Three-quarters of families in the South did not own slaves. Write three-quarters as a per cent. _____

8. Divide the circle to show the proportion of slave owners to non-slave owners in the South.

9. Vermont abolished slavery in 1777. The last Northern state to do so was New York in 1817. How many years did it take for all of the Northern states to abolish slavery?

_____

10. Harriet Tubman was born in 1820. She died in New York in 1913. How old was she when she died? _____

11. Harriet Beecher Stowe published *Uncle Tom's Cabin* in 1852. The Civil War began in 1861. How many years after she published her book did the Civil War begin?

_____

12. At first, slaves were sold very cheaply. In 1638 the price for an African male slave was about $27. In contrast, a White worker was paid about 70 cents a day.

    a. How much would a White worker be paid per week if he worked six days a week?

    _____

    b. How many weeks of pay would it take to equal $27? _____

Name:_____ Date:_____

Scavenger Hunt

Use the Internet and other reference sources to find the answers to these questions.

1. She was called Harriet when she was older, but Harriet Tubman's parents gave her a different name when she was born. They nicknamed her "Minty." What did they name her?

    _____

2. Who said these words in a speech in 1858? "A house divided against itself cannot stand … I believe this government cannot endure permanently half slave and half free."

    _____

3. Eli Whitney, inventor of the cotton gin, was born in Mulberry Grove. In what state is Mulberry Grove?

    _____

4. The first independent Methodist church for Blacks was founded in Philadelphia in 1794 by a former slave. He later became the first bishop of the African Methodist Episcopal Church. What was his name?

    _____

5. A Spanish ship sailed from Havana, Cuba, in 1839 with 54 Black slaves. Led by Joseph Cinqué, the slaves revolted, took over the ship, and attempted to sail back to Africa. They were captured by a U.S. Navy ship. A court battle followed. What was the name of the ship?

    _____

Joseph Cinqué

6. In the trial that followed the capture of the ship, the court decided the Blacks had been illegally captured and set them free. What former U.S. President was the lawyer who defended the Blacks?

    _____

7. This American poet published his book of abolitionist poetry, *Ballads and Anti-Slavery Poems,* in 1838. Included were poems titled "The Hunters of Men," "The Slave Ships," and "The Moral Welfare." What was this poet's name?

    _____

8. In 1854 it cost the U.S. government at least $100,000 to return one fugitive slave to the South. Because of the huge number of abolitionists at a convention in Boston, thousands of troops and police were needed when a fugitive was taken from a jail and put on a ship going back to Virginia. He was later sold to a friendly master who sold him to people in Boston and set him free. What was his name?

    _____

Name:_____ Date:_____

Order, Please

Number the events in order from 1 (first) to 10 (last). Use the time line at the beginning of this book for reference.

A. ____ A federal Fugitive Slave Act made it illegal to assist runaway slaves.

B. ____ Pennsylvania abolished slavery.

C. ____ The Massachusetts colony legalized slavery.

D. ____ According to Maryland law, if a free White woman married a slave, she and their children would be slaves for life.

E. ____ Vermont abolished slavery.

F. ____ Lincoln issued the Emancipation Proclamation.

G. ____ The importation of slaves into the United States became illegal.

H. ____ Abraham Lincoln was elected president.

I. ____ The first slaves were brought to Jamestown colony by a Dutch trader.

J. ____ The first formal protest of slavery in the Americas was signed by Pennsylvania Quakers.

K. Write two historical events that occurred **before** the Civil War.

_____

_____

_____

L. Write two historical events that occurred **after** the Civil War.

_____

_____

_____

Name:_____ Date:_____

Then and Now

Read the statements about conditions in the past. Add a statement about conditions today.

1. **Then:** In 1776, slavery was legal in all states.

   Now: _____

   _____

2. **Then:** The North and South disagreed strongly on many issues, especially slavery.

   Now: _____

   _____

3. **Then:** Some people were forced into slavery as a form of punishment or because they could not pay their debts.

   Now: _____

   _____

4. **Then:** Prisoners of war were forced to be slaves.

   Now: _____

   _____

5. **Then:** The Declaration of Independence and the U.S. Constitution did not allow women, Blacks, or Native Americans to vote.

   Now: _____

   _____

6. **Then:** Blacks were not allowed to attend the same schools and churches as Whites.

   Now: _____

   _____

7. **Then:** Abraham Lincoln was President of the United States.

   Now: _____

   _____

Name:_____ Date:_____

First Name, Last Name

Draw lines to match the first names with the last names.

1.	ABRAHAM	BROWN
2.	DRED	DOUGLASS
3.	ELIZABETH	FREEMAN
4.	FREDERICK	GARRETT
5.	HARRIET	GARRISON
6.	JOHN	LINCOLN
7.	NAT	SCOTT
8.	PHILLIS	TRUTH
9.	SOJOURNER	TUBMAN
10.	THOMAS	TURNER
11.	WILLIAM	WHEATLEY

Look up, down, backwards, forwards, and diagonally in the puzzle to find and circle the first and last names of the people listed above.

```
N C Q Z T K D T G P J V E U H S C J K Q W F Z W
E N H W Y E V L Y S Z S U L S I H Q X K B O Y K
T X H V K Y I H C A Q C G M A N U D M O A L M S
F L W O X Z Y R G P E O S F X N G Q G I Y F T A
M I E D J A J I R B B T R J T R U T H U R G Y P
S N W F F S K P N A H T S O J O U R N E R L N C
S S K W D P W V K E H X Q Q F S B S N A D V N N
J J Q P E Z Z Z W J A A M P C Y T O L V V S L C
V K A F B P C U P F B U Y J E C S F O E P B T C
L C D S I L L I H P R I T L X I K X V V L W S N
U I B W L D D B G H A X I G R O W L I N C O L N
Q R A I H K O F A J H Z B R K R E N R U T H E A
C E J Y I D C L R J A K A F D X M C T D S W J A
S D R O F Y B A R B M G J S W K P V O X X F L N
F E V K M E E K E R R J J L W I L L I A M V E W
R R P M W H C T T N J M I W S P R V P C R B U P
K F H D X L H G T N M T S E G K U N U J S P I T
X F O N E R A T B V V T K A I I E J G W S T D S
O R Y A U R C U N B X W H E A T L E Y U A H H X
X E P B C N D B I R J P W X K D P K Y Z L O F E
Q E M N A T G M L O A H R K V M M R D C G M J U
N M Y P R N U A J W E A T Q N D H Z W M U A U M
U A V A F E O N A N Z X Z A N S G H C X O S X G
M N E K M U Y Q Y K O F T E T N C Y S X D A O S
```

Learn More About …

Learn more about one of the people listed below who had an impact on slavery in the United States. Use the Internet and other reference sources to write a three- to five-page report. Add illustrations and maps if appropriate.

**Ellen Craft
(disguised as a man)**

Josiah Henson

Lucretia Mott

Elijah Anderson
Henry Brown
John Brown
Anthony Burns
George Washington Carver
Levi Coffin
Ellen Craft
Jefferson Davis
Frederick Douglass
Daniel Drayton
Margaret Garner
Thomas Garrett
Leonard Andrew Grimes
Josiah (Si) Henson
Udney Hyde
Jane Lewis
Elijah Lovejoy
John Malvin
John Mason
Lucretia Mott
Solomon Northup
Gabriel Prosser
Robert Purvis
John Rankin
Alexander Ross
Dred Scott
William Still
Harriet Beecher Stowe
Sojourner Truth
Harriet Tubman
Nat Turner
Phillis Wheatley

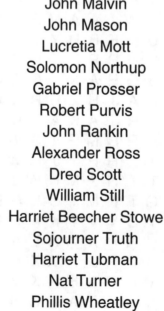

Robert Purvis

Suggested Reading

Slave Songs of the United States collected and compiled by William Francis Allen

North by Night: A Story of the Underground Railroad by Katherine Ayers

Harpers Ferry: The Story of John Brown's Raid by Tracy Barret

The Underground Railroad by Raymond Bial

The Truth About the Man Behind the Book that Sparked the War Between the States by Frances Cavanah

Slavery and the Coming of the Civil War by Christopher and James Lincoln Collier

The Last Safe House: A Story of the Underground Railroad by Barbara Greenwood

Bound for Africa: The Forced Migration of Africans to the New World by James Haskins and Kathleen Benson

Get On Board: The Story of the Underground Railroad by Jim Haskins

The Dred Scott Case: Slavery and Citizenship by D. J. Herda

Black Cargo by Richard Howard

If You Traveled on the Underground Railroad by Ellen Levine

Rebels Against Slavery: American Slave Revolts by Patricia MacKissack

They Came in Chains: The Story of the Slave Ships by Milton Meltzer

Slavery: Past and Present by Roy Pinney

Freedom Train by Dorothy Sterling

Suggested Reading

Biographies and Autobiographies

The Story of Harriet Beecher Stowe by Maureen Ash

John Brown: Antislavery Activist by Helaine Becker

Frederick Douglass Fights for Freedom by Margaret Davidson

Escape from Slavery: The Boyhood of Frederick in His Own Words by Frederick Douglass

John Brown: One Man Against Slavery by Gwen Everett

Mumbet: The Story of Elizabeth Freeman by Harold W. Felton

Go Free or Die: A Story About Harriet Tubman by Jeri Ferris

Walking the Road to Freedom: A Story About Sojourner Truth by Jeri Ferris

Phillis Wheatley: First African-American Poet by Carol Greene

Anthony Burns: The Defeat and Triumph of a Fugitive Slave by Virginia Hamilton

Harriet and the Runaway Book: The Story of Harriet Beecher Stowe and Uncle Tom's Cabin by Johanna Johnston

The Man Who Bought Himself: The Story of Peter Still by Peggy Mann and Vivian Siegal

Runaway Slave: The Story of Harriet Tubman by Ann McGovern

Sojourner Truth: A Self-Made Woman by Victoria Ortiz

Journey to Freedom: Frederick Douglass by John Passaro

Harriet Tubman: Conductor on the Underground Railroad by Ann Petry

Escape From Slavery: Five Journeys to Freedom by Doreen Rappaport

Harriet Tubman by John Rowley

Harriet Ross Tubman by Dan Troy

From Slavery to Abolitionist: The Life Of William Wells Brown adapted by Lucille Schulberg Warner

Black Crusaders for Freedom edited by Bennet Wayne

Answer Keys

A Historical View of Slavery (page 5)
3. Retribution: a penalty or punishment for doing something wrong

Life Aboard a Slave Ship (page 7)
inhumane, terrifying, filthy, cruel, atrocious, dreadful

Slavery in the South (page 9)
1. Eli Whitney
2. It was a machine that cleaned cotton (removed the seeds) much faster than could be done by hand.
3. Racism: the belief that one race is superior to another

The Declaration of Independence (page 11)
1. Unalienable: rights given by God
2. Endowed: granted, as a gift

The Constitution of the United States (page 12)
1. Controversial: something that many people disagree about
2. Compromise: an agreement between two people or groups in which each gives up something

The Fugitive Slave Laws (page 14)
1. Fugitive: a runaway; a person fleeing legal authority

Meet John Brown (page 21)
1. Arsenal: a place where weapons are made and stored
2. Treason: betrayal, usually of one's country

The Kansas-Nebraska Act (page 26)
3. 1861
4. free

Similes and Metaphors (page 28)
1. M   2. S   3. M   4. S   5. S

Meet Sojourner Truth (page 30)
1. Sojourner: a person who stays in one place for only a short time; a traveler
2. Illiterate: unable to read or write

Meet Frederick Douglass (page 34)
2. Crusade: a movement or campaign to accomplish an important goal

Uncle Tom's Cabin (page 38)
1. Serial: A long story or article, divided up into chapters or sections, and published in a magazine, one chapter or section at a time.

Fact or Opinion? (page 39)
1. F   6. O
2. F   7. F
3. O   8. F
4. O   9. O
5. F   10. O

The Union Is Divided (page 44)
1. Students should color the states listed.
2. Students should color all other states, but not territories. Be certain they indicate that California and Oregon were also part of the Union.
3. Oklahoma
4. Territories: Washington, Dakota, Nebraska, Utah, Nevada, Colorado, New Mexico

Jefferson Davis or Abraham Lincoln? (page 46)
1. JD   5. AL   9. AL   13. JD
2. BOTH   6. JD   10. JD   14. BOTH
3. AL   7. JD   11. AL   15. JD
4. AL   8. BOTH   12. JD

The Emancipation Proclamation (page 47)
1. no
4. Fifteenth
5. 1870
6. Nineteenth
7. 1920

Matching (page 48)
1. illiterate
2. compromise
3. sojourner
4. abolitionists
5. Harriet Beecher Stowe
6. Harriet Tubman
7. retribution
8. arsenal
9. treason
10. emancipation
11. John Brown
12. Abraham Lincoln
13. Jefferson Davis
14. fugitive
15. inhumane
16. Frederick Douglass

True or False? (page 50)
1. F   5. T   9. T   13. F
2. F   6. T   10. T   14. F
3. T   7. F   11. F   15. T
4. T   8. F   12. F

Figuratively Speaking (page 52)

Exact answers will vary, but should be similar to the following.

1. Very forcefully or strictly
2. From one bad situation to another
3. Postponing until a later time
4. Headed in as straight a line as possible
5. Made returning impossible
6. A fantasy or dream
7. Something that cuts both directions; both hurt and helped
8. Increased; aroused

Historical Math (page 53)

1. 142 years
2. 11 years
3. 31
4. 40 years
5. 20
6. 600,000
7. 75%
8. graph should show 75% non-slave owners and 25% slave owners
9. 40 years
10. 93
11. 9 years
12a. $4.20
12b. about 6.4 weeks

Scavenger Hunt (page 54)

1. Araminta (Ross)
2. Abraham Lincoln
3. Georgia
4. Richard Allen
5. *Amistad*
6. John Quincy Adams
7. John Greenleaf Whittier
8. Anthony Burns

Order, Please (page 55)

A.	7	F.	10
B.	6	G.	8
C.	2	H.	9
D.	3	I.	1
E.	5	J.	4

First Name, Last Name (page 57)

1. ABRAHAM LINCOLN
2. DRED SCOTT
3. ELIZABETH FREEMAN
4. FREDERICK DOUGLASS
5. HARRIET TUBMAN
6. JOHN BROWN
7. NAT TURNER
8. PHILLIS WHEATLEY
9. SOJOURNER TRUTH
10. THOMAS GARRETT
11. WILLIAM GARRISON

Word Search Puzzle (page 57)

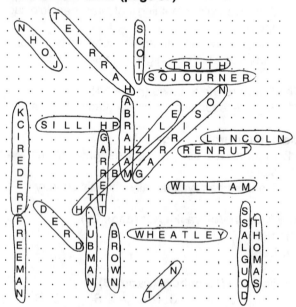